JUNGLE
ANIMAL GROUPS

by
Rebecca Phillips-Bartlett

Minneapolis, Minnesota

Credits
All images are courtesy of Shutterstock.com, unless otherwise specified. With thanks to Getty Images, Thinkstock Photo, and iStockphoto. Recurring images – imaginasty, Alexander A. Nedviga, abakeagle, Ihor Biliavskyi, oxy_gen. Cover – Eric Isslee, PUMPZA, GUDKOV ANDREY, Charlotte Bleijenberg, sweet kiwi, SaveJungle, Oleksandra Klestova. 2–3 – Lucia Fox, Natalia Paklina. 4–5 – Ondrej Prosicky, Sukma Rizqi, Mary Ann McDonald, BlackFarm. 6–7 – PeterBatarseh, SaveJungle, STILLFX, Teo Tarras. 8–9 – Alfmaler, daraka, Davefoc (Wikimedia Commons), Pavel Krasensky, Watthana Boonwarn. 10–11 – Maquiladora, Mendesbio, Oleksandra Klestova. 12–13 – dcaillat, GUDKOV ANDREY, NotionPic, Sergey Uryadnikov. 14–15 – CXI, GUDKOV ANDREY, Guz Anna, Ondrej Prosicky. 16–17 – dangdumrong, Macrovector, Ondrej Prosicky, Savrah Cheriton-Jones. 18–19 – Charlotte Bleijenberg, Hajakely, Miroslav Halama, Mvshop, Ondrej Chvatal. 20–21 – Flow 37, Giedriius, JT Platt, Lukiyanova Natalia frenta, Ondrej Prosicky, Sketchart. 22–23 – Michael Neue, Natalia Kuzmina, SIN1980.

Bearport Publishing Company Product Development Team
President: Jen Jenson; Director of Product Development: Spencer Brinker; Managing Editor: Allison Juda; Associate Editor: Naomi Reich; Associate Editor: Tiana Tran; Senior Designer: Colin O'Dea; Associate Designer: Elena Klinkner; Associate Designer: Kayla Eggert; Product Development Assistant: Owen Hamlin

Library of Congress Cataloging-in-Publication Data

Names: Phillips-Bartlett, Rebecca, 1999- author.
Title: Jungle animal groups / Rebecca Phillips-Bartlett.
Description: Minneapolis, Minnesota : Bearport Publishing Company, [2024] | Series: Wild animal families | Includes index.
Identifiers: LCCN 2023029021 (print) | LCCN 2023029022 (ebook) | ISBN 9798889163237 (library binding) | ISBN 9798889163282 (paperback) | ISBN 9798889163329 (ebook)
Subjects: LCSH: Jungle animals--Polar regions--Juvenile literature.
Classification: LCC QL112 .P49 2024 (print) | LCC QL112 (ebook) | DDC 591.730911--dc23/eng/20230713
LC record available at https://lccn.loc.gov/2023029021
LC ebook record available at https://lccn.loc.gov/2023029022

© 2024 BookLife Publishing
This edition is published by arrangement with BookLife Publishing.

North American adaptations © 2024 Bearport Publishing Company. All rights reserved. No part of this publication may be reproduced in whole or in part, stored in any retrieval system, or transmitted in any form or by any means, electronic, mechanical, photocopying, recording, or otherwise, without written permission from the publisher.

For more information, write to Bearport Publishing, 5357 Penn Avenue South, Minneapolis, MN 55419.

CONTENTS

Wild Animal Families.......... 4
In the Jungle 6
Ants 8
Vampire Bats 10
Bonobos 12
Mountain Gorillas............ 14
Tigers 16
Ring-Tailed Lemurs.......... 18
Toucans 20
Family Focus................. 22
Glossary 24
Index 24

WILD ANIMAL FAMILIES

Earth is full of amazing animals. Many of them live in groups. This helps animals stay safe. It also makes it easier for them to find food and a place to stay.

Let's visit different animal families in the jungle. This **habitat** has everything the plants and animals there need to live.

Many different wild animals make their homes in jungles.

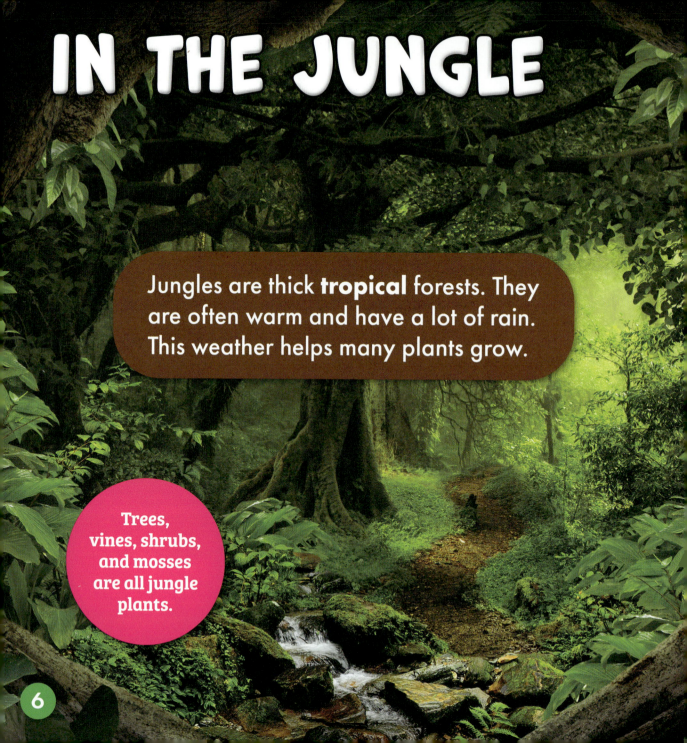

IN THE JUNGLE

Jungles are thick **tropical** forests. They are often warm and have a lot of rain. This weather helps many plants grow.

Trees, vines, shrubs, and mosses are all jungle plants.

Most jungles can be found around the middle of Earth. Jungles grow in the Americas, Africa, and Asia. Different jungles are home to different kinds of plant and animal life.

ANTS

Ants in the jungle live in large groups called colonies. Most ant colonies have one queen and thousands of worker ants.

The queen ant is bigger than the worker ants.

Queen ant

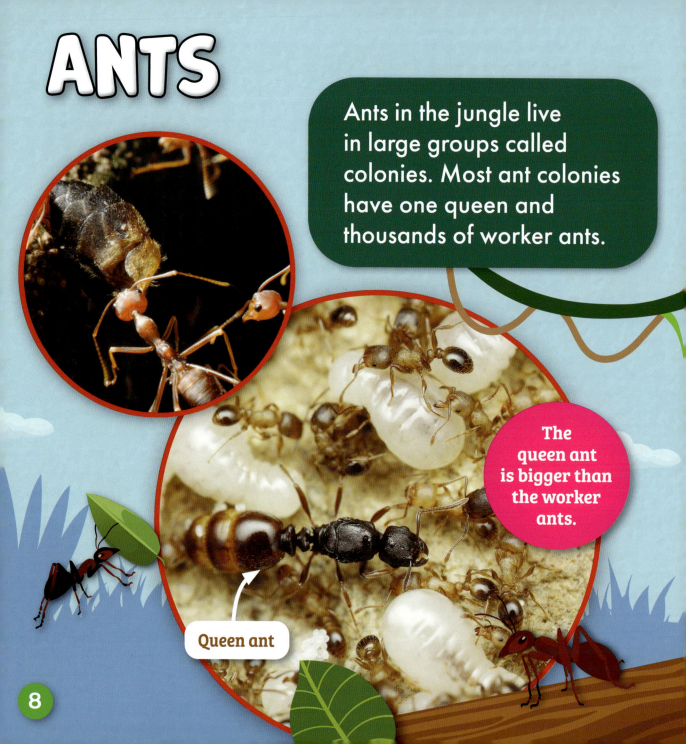

Ant colonies are known for their teamwork. Worker ants come together to build a home and find food. Sometimes, they even climb on one another to get from place to place.

Worker ants

VAMPIRE BATS

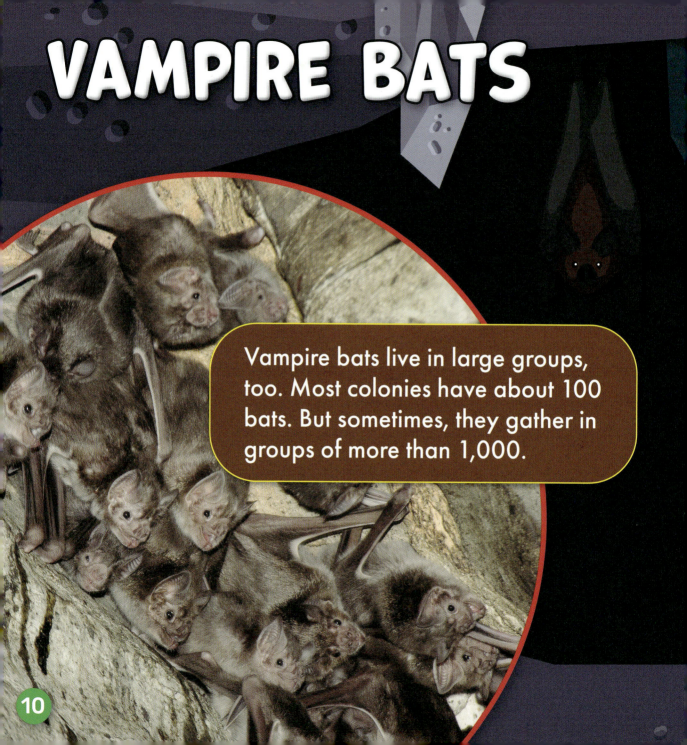

Vampire bats live in large groups, too. Most colonies have about 100 bats. But sometimes, they gather in groups of more than 1,000.

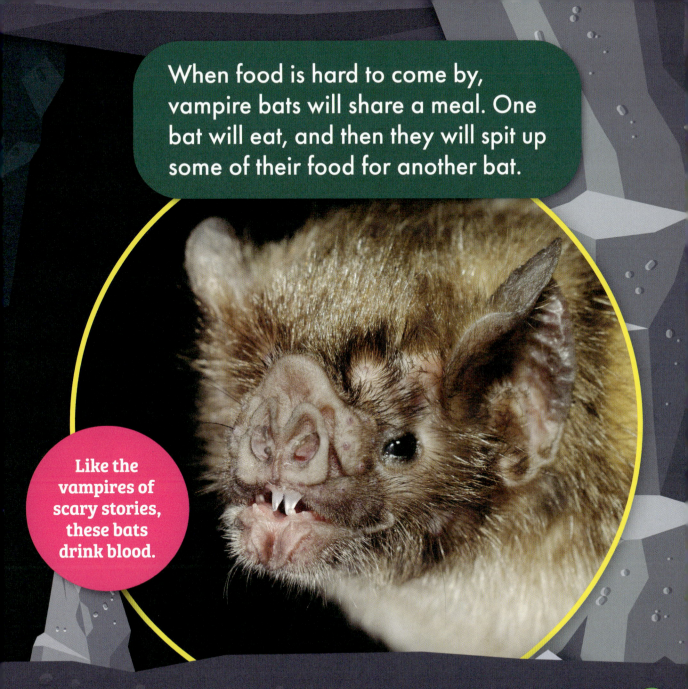

When food is hard to come by, vampire bats will share a meal. One bat will eat, and then they will spit up some of their food for another bat.

Like the vampires of scary stories, these bats drink blood.

BONOBOS

Bonobos live in **female**-led groups called troops. During the day, these troops split into smaller groups to look for food.

Bonobos eat fruits and leaves.

Bonobo groups **bond** together when mothers give birth. The ties between mothers and babies are the strongest. But others bonobos help the mother, connecting the larger group, too.

MOUNTAIN GORILLAS

Like bonobos, mountain gorillas also live in troops. However, gorilla troops are very different. These groups are led by an older **male** gorilla.

The male leading a mountain gorilla troop is called a silverback.

Young gorillas learn from the troop. At first, they get everything from their mothers. As they grow, they start to copy other older gorillas to learn what to do, too.

TIGERS

Tigers live in small family groups when their babies are young. Tiger cubs learn how to hunt from their mothers. After two years, the young tigers leave the group.

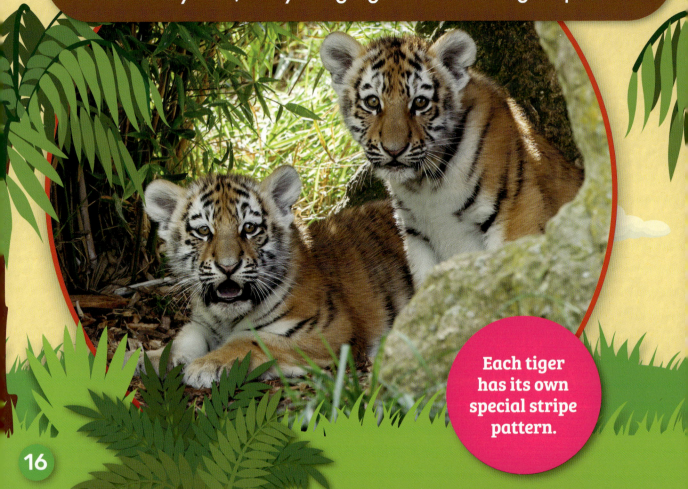

Each tiger has its own special stripe pattern.

At this point, tigers grow and live alone. When they are ready to have babies, they form family groups of their own.

RING-TAILED LEMURS

Groups of ring-tailed lemurs know how to stick together. The furry animals keep their tails in the air when they walk. This helps the lemurs keep track of one another so they do not get lost.

Ring-tailed lemurs are named after their striped tails.

Lemurs **grooming** each other

Lemurs use their teeth to groom themselves and other lemurs. This keeps them clean and forms strong bonds.

TOUCANS

Toucans travel by hopping between branches.

Toucans live in small groups called flocks. These birds live at the very top of the trees in the jungle.

Toucans make the most of their jungle habitat. Instead of building new nests, toucans often live in nests made by other birds.

Toucan nest

FAMILY FOCUS

Many amazing animal family groups live in the jungle. These groups are all different in many ways. However, they do have some things in common.

Working together helps animals face the many **challenges** of their jungle habitats. They teach their young, hunt for food, and find safe places to live.

Which animal family group would you like to join?

GLOSSARY

bond a close connection

challenges difficult problems or tasks that require extra effort

female an animal that can give birth or lay eggs

grooming cleaning fur or skin

habitat a place in nature where a plant or animal normally lives

male an animal that cannot give birth or lay eggs

tropical having to do with the warm areas near the middle of Earth

INDEX

colonies 8–10
flocks 20–21
food 4, 9, 11–12, 23
groups 4, 8, 12–13, 16–18, 20, 22–23

habitat 5, 21, 23
hunt 16, 23
queen ants 8

silverback gorillas 14
troops 12, 14–15